# Words of Power

## Secret Magickal Sounds That Manifest Your Desires

**DAMON BRAND**

THE GALLERY OF MAGICK

Copyright © 2015 Damon Brand

All Rights Reserved. This book may not be reproduced, in whole or in part, in any form or by any means electronic or mechanical, including photocopying, recording, or by any information storage retrieval system now known or hereafter invented, without written permission from the publisher, The Gallery of Magick.

*It is hereby expressly stated that the images in this book may not be reproduced in any form, except for individual and personal use. Derivative works based on these images or the associated concepts are not permitted, and any such attempt to create a derivative work will be met with legal action.*

Disclaimer: Consider all information in this book to be speculation and not professional advice, to be used at your own risk. Damon Brand and The Gallery of Magick are not responsible for the consequences of your actions should you choose to use the methods in this book. Success depends on the integrity of your workings, the initial conditions of your life and your natural abilities so results will vary. The information is never intended to replace or substitute for medical advice from a professional practitioner, and when it comes to issues of physical health, mental health or emotional conditions, no advice is given or implied, and you should always seek conventional, professional advice. The information is provided on the understanding that you will use it in accordance with the laws of your country.

# CONTENTS

| | |
|---|---|
| How the Magick Works | 7 |
| Why Magick is Safe and Fair | 9 |
| How to Pronounce the Words | 11 |
| How to Use Words of Power | 15 |
| Using the Words in Urgent Situations | 19 |
| After the Magick | 21 |
| Activating the Words of Power | 23 |
| | |
| The Words of Power | 27 |
| To Win an Argument | 28 |
| To Win a Competition | 30 |
| End Bad Luck | 32 |
| Protection from Violence | 34 |
| Make Somebody Kinder | 36 |
| Make Your Money Go Further | 38 |
| Attract Generosity from Others | 40 |
| Make a Project Go Viral | 42 |
| Get Public Support for a Project | 44 |
| Dedicate Yourself to a New Skill | 46 |
| Obtain Wisdom | 48 |
| Know What Somebody is Thinking | 50 |
| Learn About the Near Future | 52 |
| Learn About the Far Future | 54 |
| Become the Most Loveable Version of Yourself | 56 |
| Feel More Self-Respect | 58 |
| Be the Center of Attention | 60 |
| Have Your Talent Recognized | 62 |
| Appear Valuable to Somebody of Importance | 64 |
| Attract a Guide or Mentor | 66 |
| Be Given a Chance, Against the Odds | 68 |
| Let Go of Guilt and Shame | 70 |
| Make an Enemy Terrified of You | 72 |
| Make More Time Become Available | 74 |
| Gain an Advantage, Obtain Any Desire or Find Favor | 76 |
| When the Magick Works | 79 |
| | |
| Appendix A: What the Words Mean | 81 |

# How the Magick Works

Words of Power work because they give you access to angelic forces that connect with divine power.

If you have a sincere desire, speaking these words can make the magick come alive for you. Of all the systems I have worked with, this is the easiest to use and has often brought the most long-lasting results.

If you've ever done magick of any kind – whether casting a spell, performing a ritual or even just praying – this may sound too good to be true. I felt the same way when I first explored these ideas because I have spent a lot of time working with more complex magick. When I tried the Words of Power, the results I received convinced me that this magick works.

It takes moments to read the words or phrases, and then the magick happens.

The words used are a combination of divine names and angelic names, but knowing the words is only part of the process. In developing this magick, the most vital aspect was finding the right word *combinations* to access magick. I work with a group known as The Gallery of Magick, and we spent several decades testing the best combinations to create the most effective Words of Power.

This book provides twenty-five magickal word combinations that produce specific and powerful results. To me, magick is about getting results in the real world, and that is the promise of this book.

Words of Power can be used by experienced occultists to add extra power to their work, or by complete beginners. It is one of the most accessible systems we've ever created because it requires nothing other than your eyes, your mind, and your voice. All you need is to scan over the words with your eyes and vocalize the sounds. If you're in a rush, or in public, you can whisper or think a shortened version of the words.

You can use the Words of Power by themselves and you will get results. If you are using other magick rituals, you can use these words to add extra direction and energy to your workings.

You can scan through the book and find a chapter you want to use, but I advise against this. Although this is the fastest form of magick I know, it works best when activated by a simple ritual. This activation ritual is a way of giving you a direct and intentional connection to the Words of Power. It is simple to perform and takes only minutes. After that, you can use any ritual you want.

Your pronunciation does *not* have to be perfect, but you will get much better results if you are relaxed about saying the words. A little practice will help you relax.

Many people worry about pronunciation, so I've made this as simple as possible, and if you follow my guidance, you'll get close enough for the magick to work. All the words are spelled phonetically, so it's just like reading English. Better still, the book is Pronunciation Proof, because you scan the words visually before you say them. There's also a video/audio guide on the website to make everything completely clear.

Rather than skimming through to the Words of Power themselves, please read all the instructions that come before them to get the best results.

Before using a particular section, it helps to read the whole book and learn what each set of words can do. You may find that there's a better solution to your problem than the one you might have picked first.

Take this small amount of time to prepare, and the book will reward you for many years to come.

# Why Magick is Safe and Fair

People often ask if magick is safe. In certain conditions, magick can be dangerous, but *this* magick has been designed with safety in mind. You are calling on divine powers to work through angelic beings to align your reality with your sincere desire. There is no danger in that.

When magick starts to work for people, they sometimes worry that they have an unfair advantage in the world, or that there may be a backlash and that they'll be punished with bad luck. This is not the case. You will have an advantage, but there are no adverse side effects.

Sometimes, when people perform particularly violent curses, their guilt attracts bad luck, and this has led to a widespread belief that magick always rebounds in some way. This is not true. The magick itself does not punish you.

Angels are messengers, and it is their duty to perform the tasks we ask them to perform – without judgment - when we ask. As such, you will not be punished for your success.

Thankfully, you don't need to believe anything, but you should act as though magickal results are *possible*, and be enthusiastic about the magick Remain open to the possibility of results, rather than doubting the system, and you will get results. Although I talk of rapid results, patience is one of the greatest occult skills, and the more patient you are, the faster you get what you want.

You may also wonder why there's so much Hebrew text in the book. Some readers are concerned that without a Western or Judeo-Christian background, this magick won't work. Thankfully, the magick even works for atheists, and people from all other religions that we know about, so this is not a problem.

The Hebrew words are a shortcut that help us to access the angels. Although this means working on pronunciation a little, the words are all spelled phonetically, so it's not a problem. You don't have to learn Hebrew or ever know what the words mean. You only need to know that you are calling on divine powers and angelic beings to assist you. (If you want to know what the words mean, see Appendix A at the end of the book.)

For the magick to work, please make sure you read this book thoroughly, and take the time to choose the results you want carefully. This magick can perform seeming miracles, but you will get the best results if you work patiently, slowly building up the results. If you aim for an instant lottery win, don't be surprised when the magick doesn't work. Take your time, understand what the magick can do for you, and seek the results that will serve you best.

Read everything I have to say about 'lust for result,' to ensure that you aren't yearning or longing for results. The more patient and confident you are, the faster results come. If you look for results or test the system, it is less likely to work. Instead, approach this system with serious intent, but a playful confidence, as though results are inevitable. If you can do that, you will unlock the magick rapidly.

# How to Pronounce the Words

Pronunciation of these words is easy. I'll explain it all in this chapter, but if you can go online, have a look at the *Pronunciation and Spelling FAQ* at **www.galleryofmagick.com** because there's an audio/video guide that makes this all much easier.

If you only have the book, then you read the words that are in capital letters as though they are written in English.

For example, the word Adiriron is pronounced as:

### ADD-EAR-EAR-ON

ADD sounds like the word you use when you *add* up a score. EAR sounds like the *ear* on the side of your head. And ON sounds like the word you use to switch *on* a light.

Although this is extremely simple, it's worth reading through the words a few times to get used to their sound before using them in a ritual.

Some of the sounds are a little more obscure. For example:

### EH-YEAH

EH sounds like the *e* sound in *bet*.

YEAH sounds exactly as you'd imagine – the slang way of saying yes in English or American English. 'Oh *yeah*!'

If it looks like an English word, just read it as an English word. This applies to words such as ADD, AIR, ARE, ASH, ASS, AT, BAR, CAR, EAR, EBB, GIVE, GORE, HAT, HAY, ME, NAG, ON, OR, PACK, PAIR, SHE, SHOO, TEE, TWO, YEAH, YELL and WHO.

For the rest, this guide might help:

### G

G always sound like the *g* in *guess* rather than the *g* in *gem*.

## AH

AH sounds like that *a* sound in **father**. It can also be compared to the *a* sound in *ma* and *pa*.

## A

There is also a shorter *a* sound. For example, **NA** is like *nap* without the *p*. Wherever you see a syllable end with *a*, rather than *ah*, it is this short *a* sound. This is based on the way the English would say words such as *nap*, *lap*, and *map*, with a slightly shorter **a** than in American English. Precision is, however, not required.

## EH

EH is like the middle part of the word *bet*. Say *bet* without the *b* or the *t* and you've got **EH**.

## UH

UH is *up* without the *p*. If you see the sound **YUH**, you know that it sounds like *yuk* without the *k*. **DUH** is like *duck* without the *ck*.

## YAH

YAH is included in many of these words, so note that **YAH** is *ah* with *y* at the front. It's like *yarn* without the *rn*.

## AW

AW is like *awe* or *raw* without the *r*. If you see **BAW**, you know it sounds like the word *awe* with *b* at the beginning.

## TZ

TZ is the sound you get at the end of words such as *cats*, *bats*, and *rats*.

## AY

AY is like *pay* without the *p*.

## CH

CH presents more of a challenge as it is meant to sound like the guttural *ch* in the Scottish *loch* or the German *achtung*. You may find our online audio guide useful when it comes to this sound. If you struggle at all, replace every **CH** with **K**. A sound such as **CHEE** becomes **KEE**. This is better than becoming overly frustrated. If you are willing to learn the correct **CH** sound, it is a satisfying way to make the words flow together.

You can't get it wrong. If you see **BAH**, you now know that's the **AH** sound with *b* at the front. If you see **CHAHSH**, you now know that's the **CH** sound, followed by the **AH** sound, ending with **SH**. It's not difficult if you take each word slowly, and it gets easier with a little practice.

To be relaxed about pronunciation, take a few minutes to practice the sounds before you begin so that you can say them with ease and flow when you perform the ritual. Feeling comfortable is far more important than getting the sounds objectively correct.

One reason that the written words appear in Hebrew, inside a boxed sigil, is so that your pronunciation is far less important. When you scan over the words visually, before saying them aloud, *more than half the magick has been done.* You don't need to understand a word of Hebrew. You look at the words, and *that* activates the connection. This makes the book Pronunciation Proof.

Do not worry about pronunciation. I cannot state this strongly enough. Even though pronunciation may *seem* essential, it is not. Nothing is worse for your magick than worrying about getting it precisely correct. It's better to do magick often and with bold intent than to aim for perfection.

I used to get people asking me about pronunciation all the time, but unless I know your voice, where you live, where you were brought up, your education level and what languages you speak, I probably can't give you any better advice than is presented in this book. Read the words as though they are plain English and you'll be doing it exactly right. If you ever have a concern, check back on this chapter or watch the video on the website.

You can trust that many people have tested our pronunciations, and they work.

# How to Use Words of Power

When you perform magick, it is usually to solve a problem or to speed up a result that you already expect. Magick can also be used to enhance qualities in yourself and to experience psychic intuition.

If you've purchased this book, you probably know what your problems are and the solutions you want. Make sure you've read through all the descriptions of the Words of Power, and then choose the chapter that will solve your problem best.

If you think it will help to use several chapters at once, go ahead. In general, I'd be wary of using more than three different chapters at once, as this can muddy the waters. It's better to be precise and powerful than to throw all the magick you can at a problem.

If you've been experiencing a run of bad luck with money, and you're struggling to pay the bills, then you might use *End Bad Luck* and *Make Your Money Go Further*. If you feel you need more help from family, because they have been ungenerous of late, you could work on *Attract Generosity from Others* at the same time.

First, be certain to perform the ritual in the chapter *Activating the Words of Power*.

When you have done that, and chosen the chapter relevant to your problem, do the following:

Sit in a quiet place. Consider your problem, and think about what you want to change. Mull over the problem and how it makes you feel.

Now scan each word in the sigil, looking at the letters silently from right to left. This is the opposite way to reading standard English because Hebrew is read from right to left. Start with the uppermost word and work your way down the list. You do not need to do anything other than see the word. You're not reading but *scanning* the letters. You're letting them sink into your consciousness, and that is enough.

If there are two lists, start with the list on the right. When you get to the bottom of that list, read the list on the left from top to bottom. As always, each word should be scanned from right to left.

Now think of how grateful you would feel if your problem was solved. You should *not* try to think of the solution itself, but think of how you would *feel* if the problem went away. At the beginning of the ritual, you wondered about your problem, so now you should ponder the feeling you'd get if the problem were no longer a reality.

If you want to end bad luck, don't think of all the things that need to happen to end the bad luck. Don't try to problem solve. Instead, think about the relief you would feel if your dream came true. This skill is important, so make sure you get it right. Never try to solve the problem for the spirits by thinking about the details, but think of how you will feel when it is solved *for you*.

Once you have that feeling of relief and gratitude, as though the result has already happened, you are sending a clear emotional message to the angels, and they know what you want to feel. They can make that feeling come true.

All you have to do now is speak the Words of Power. These are written below each box, and they are read as standard English, from left to right.

If you are alone and can say them loudly, then let the words vibrate through your throat. It's as though you are breathing the words out, letting them rumble up from your belly through the back of your throat. It's almost as though you are chanting or singing them.

This 'vibration', where you let the words rumble out of you is not essential and will be impossible for many, so if need be, just say them out loud.

How you say the words is less important than the feeling you have when you speak. Remember that every word is a divine name or a connection to a spirit that works the will of the divine. Each time you say a word, speak *as though you are speaking to a spirit*.

This doesn't mean you need to pray or beg or plead – in fact, quite the opposite. You are charging the spirits to do your bidding, but it's important to say the words *to* somebody. Imagine what happens when you call your friend's name. You are not simply saying a word; you are calling a name *to* your friend. The same should be true of every Word of Power. Make it feel as though you are sending your feeling of gratitude out to each name you call.

To be clear, each line contains a single Word of Power. So, ADD-EAR-EAR-ON is one word of power. LAV is another Word of Power, and so on. Each line gives you a new Word of Power, and each should be spoken with the feeling of gratitude, *to* the being you are calling on.

Between each word, you may want to glance at the sigil. You don't have to scan the words, but see the sigil if you can, for a moment.

Sometimes you may sense a response from the spirits, but often you will feel nothing. It doesn't matter, so long as you hold on to the feeling of gratitude as you say the words.

That is the entire technique. When you have said the final word, you can close the book and go about your business. Try not to think about the results or how they will come about. Look at the articles on The Gallery of Magick website for details on 'lust for result' to ensure you don't short circuit the magick, and you'll get what you want. Results can be instant, or they can take time. *Let them come when they come.*

You only need to perform the ritual once, but if, after a few days, you feel a strong urge to repeat the ritual, you can. There is no harm in performing it every day if it makes you feel better, but I prefer to use it once with real commitment, concentration, and enjoyment. Never repeat the ritual due to doubts or fears that it hasn't worked, because your trust and patience is essential. Only repeat if you feel an intuitive desire to do so.

When performing the ritual, you only need to read the words once. The only exception to this is the Activation ritual, where you speak one set of words three times. Other than that, stick to one read-through.

If you need to perform your magick in silence, for the sake of privacy or any other reason, you can do so. Some people whisper the words, and others say them in their heads. Either method works so long as you imagine you are calling the names to the ends of the Universe. This is one reason why silence can actually be better than whispering because you can imagine that you're calling the words out like a mighty being, but if you whisper, it can make the words seem quiet and small. Choose a method that you're comfortable with and it will work.

# Using the Words in Urgent Situations

The previous chapter described the ideal way to carry out the magick, but the beauty of Words of Power is that they can be used in emergency situations. This does take some preparation, but it works.

Imagine you have to pass through a rough and dangerous area during your day. This happened to me some time ago. I was staying in an interesting part of a city and had to pass through a place that was regarded as a no-go area for many. It was unnerving and could be quite dangerous. I had the option of taking a cab or driving through, but I preferred to walk, so I decided that I *would* walk. I used magick to ensure that for the ten minutes spent passing through the rough area, each day, I would be safe.

I performed the ritual using the **Protection from Violence** chapter. It uses the following words.

ADD-EAR-EAR-ON
ADD-EAR-ON
TZ-UR-TAK
YEE-SHOO-HAK-OVAH-VAHA
NAFF-LEE-ELL
LAV

The beauty of this system, however, is that you only need to remember the first and last word to use it in an emergency. So, during this time, I made sure that I had ADD-EAR-EAR-ON and LAV clearly memorized. If at any time, during my walk, I felt that I was being watched, pursued or about to be attacked, I would simply say those words. Sometimes I would say them silently. Other times I would say them out loud. Once, I called them out to the face of somebody who was about to rob me. You'll know what's right depending on the circumstances. One brief call is all that's needed, so long as you've already performed the full ritual once.

In the full ritual, you need to think of your problem, feel a sense of relief at the result and call the names as though speaking to divine beings. In this 'emergency' version of the magick, you can keep it much more straightforward. All you need to remember is that your request is being heard by the spirits you are calling on. Then carry on with your walk, or whatever it is you are doing.

This system is particularly impressive because it can be used in other contexts. After I'd left that city, I found myself in danger a few times, and I used the same call. Even though I'd originally set it up to protect me in the previous city, I had learned the method, and it still worked.

Some of these chapters do not apply to emergency situations. You would not, for example, *Make a Project Go Viral* while walking down the street, or even in a business meeting. Those Words of Power are aimed at long-term projects. But you might use *Make Somebody Kinder* during dinner with your family. And you might use *Know What Somebody is Thinking* during a business meeting. Although the Words of Power can be used as described in the previous chapter, to give you a result, using them exactly when they are needed can yield amazing and instant results.

In some cases, several chapters use the same first and last word, but this doesn't stop you using them in an emergency. You may notice that *Get Public Support for a Project* and *Learn About the Near Future* both contain EH-YEAH at the beginning and HAH-RACH at the end. Thankfully, this doesn't stop you using the shortcut method. So long as *you* know why you're calling on the spirits, the magick will work. Some people also carry the sigil containing the words with them. This is not required, but you should know that it is an option and one that some magickal practitioners enjoy.

# After the Magick

When you have finished your magick, you should avoid lusting for result. You can still think about the result you want to occur, but avoid searching, hoping and praying for it to come true. Doing this can hijack the magick. Instead, act as though you are so confident in the magick that you don't need to worry.

When you do think about the result you seek, simply recreate the feeling of gratitude that the result has come to pass (as though it already has) and you open the door to results.

If results don't show up immediately, avoid saying, 'That ritual didn't work,' because impatience will never help a result to come about. You never know where and when a result may manifest, so don't assume that a ritual has failed just because you don't see instant results.

Although this magick is designed to work fast, results can sometimes occur later, when you are genuinely ready, and when you least expect it. In some cases, it may take you a while to attune to the magick. If you say that a ritual has failed, you are drawing a line under it and canceling it out. It is far better to assume that the magick will keep working, and can bring your result about at some point in the future. Most of the time, this isn't an issue, as the magick works fast.

Where you can, you should also put in some of your own effort in the real world. If you ask for **Protection from Violence**, make sure you don't shout abuse at your neighbors. If you want your talent to be recognized, work on improving your talent. Magick works best when you put in some effort of your own. That may require a little imagination. If, for example, you are using magick to improve self-esteem, take the time to sit alone with your feelings for a few minutes. That could be enough, and shows the spirits that you also have a commitment to the magick. When you are committed to the magick, so are they.

# Activating the Words of Power

On the following page, you will see a sigil designed to give you access to change and to connect you to the divine words that are used throughout this book.

This sigil, like the rest in this book, contains several pentagrams, displayed in a two-tone style. Please note that the pentagram is not evil (although Hollywood would have you believe it), but symbolizes, amongst other things, the human body, various elements, and even the five primary senses. Here, this version of the pentagram is a way of seeing *you* as an interactive part of the universe, rather than passively existing within it, and helps to give fluidity to your reality.

The following ritual needs only to be performed once, ever. After performing this ritual just once, the words are activated forever. If you feel that you made a mistake, you are free to repeat it, but in most cases, once is enough. This is what you do:

Gaze at the sigil for about a minute. Do not stare, but keep your gaze soft, and just let the patterns and lines sink into your consciousness.

Starting at the top line, scan over each word from right to left, as described earlier. You are not trying to understand, read or feel anything. You are simply letting your gaze absorb those letters.

Now speak (or vibrate) the words below the sigil, starting with UB-AH-GEE-TAHTZ.

Repeat each spoken word *three* times before moving on to the next line. You do not need to repeat the gaze and scan, only the spoken words. You will end with SHUH-KAHV-TZUH-YAHT being spoken three times.

These words are derived from The 42 Letter Name of God. By speaking them while looking at a sigil drawn in the style of the other sigils in the book, you help to create a connection to this magick. For more details on the exact meaning see *Appendix A*, but for now, it's best to ignore the theory and do the magick.

Then complete the ritual with the second sigil and the closing words, which are said just *once*.

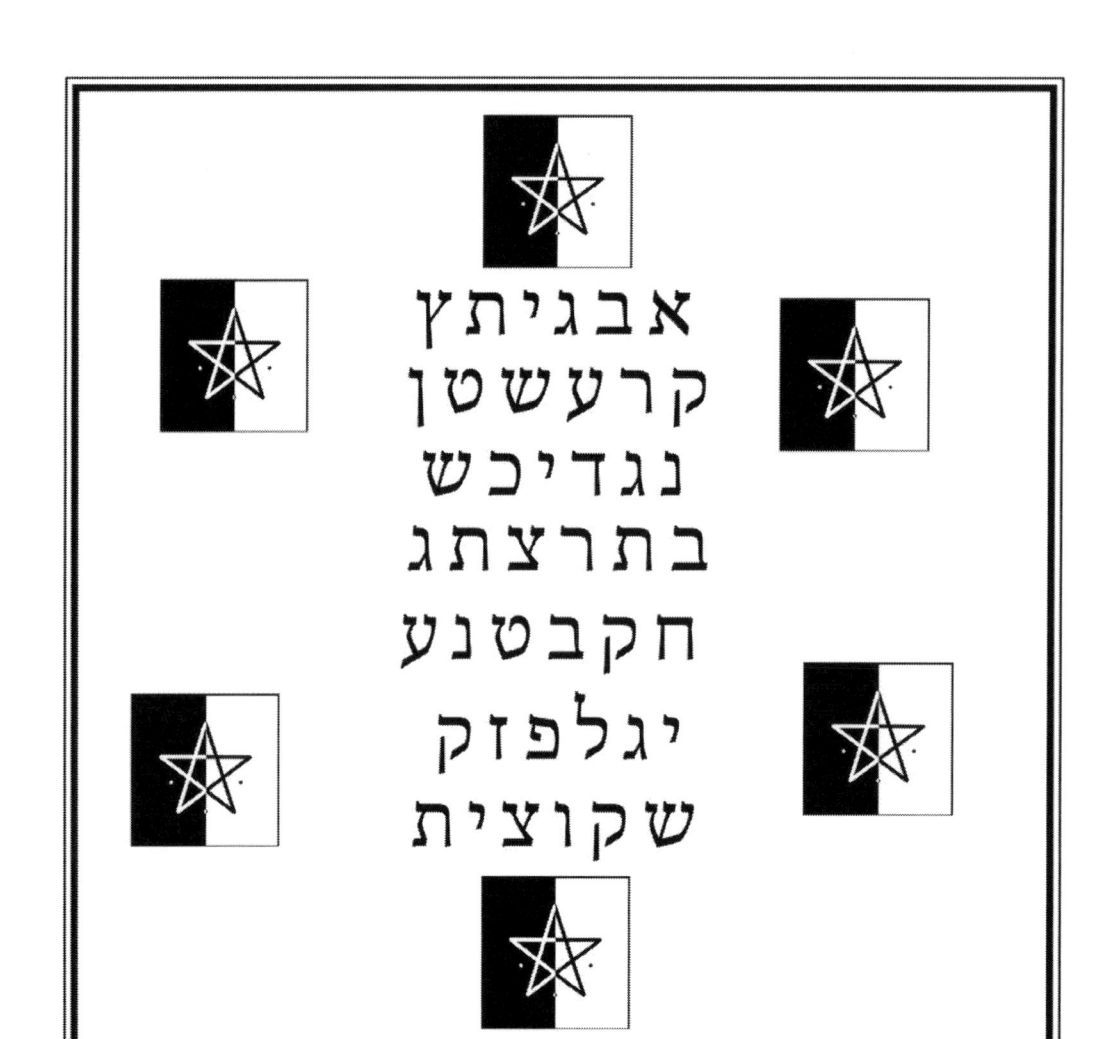

אבגיתץ
קרעשטן
נגדיכש
בתרצתג
חקבטנע
יגלפזק
שקוצית

UB-AH-GEE-TAHTZ
KUH-RAH-SUH-TAHN
NUH-GAHD-EE-CHAHSH
BUH-TAHR-TZAH-TAHG
CHUH-KAHB-TAH-NAH
YUH-GAHL-PUH-ZAHK
SHUH-KAHV-TZUH-YAHT

When you have spoken the words three times each, as described, gaze at this next sigil for a moment, and scan the words from right to left, starting at the top. Again, this is just visual scanning, not reading.

אהיה אשר אהיה

ברוך המקום

Say this once:

EH-YEAH ASH-AIR EH-YEAH

In this context, this means 'I will become what I please' or 'I will be what I will be' and is a way of connecting your will, your choices and your desires to divine power.

Finish by blessing omnipresent power, by saying this once:

BAR-UCH HAH-MAH-KOM

It is done.

As soon as you have said, 'It is done,' you are ready to use the Words of Power at once, or whenever you please.

# The Words of Power

The following pages contain descriptions of the powers, sigils for each set of words, along with the pronunciation of the words in capitals.

Remember the essential process is to consider your problem, scan the words visually, feel the emotion of your result, say the words to the spirits and then go about your day as normal.

If you are using a device such as an iPad, and find the device makes it impossible for you to see the sigil on the same page as the words, take the time to write down the spoken words on a piece of paper. This means you can keep the sigil in front of you as you speak the words. On most devices, or in the printed book, this won't be a problem. If you do use a piece of paper, it can be thrown in the trash when you are done.

When saying the words, you don't need to stare at the sigil, but it can be useful to glance at it casually between spoken words, so long as your focus stays on the emotions.

# To Win an Argument

Whether your argument is one that has raged for years with a huge corporation or a minor dispute with a family member, this is one way to win the argument peacefully.

    This can also be used to get somebody to listen to you if you feel your message isn't getting through at first.

# To Win an Argument

אדירירון
יאהבוגה
פרחיאל

ADD-EAR-EAR-ON
YEE-AH-HA-VEEV-GE-HAH
PAIR-ACH-EE-ELL

# To Win a Competition

This is not aimed at winning the lottery or other games of chance. But if you are engaged in any competition that requires your skill, from poker to the Olympics, this is one way to make sure you gain an advantage.

It can be used to win a writing competition, to win an award or even to win a particularly competitive job. Any time when you sense you are being defeated by competition, use this to enhance your skills and improve your luck.

It works less effectively for something such as sales, for example, unless you are *competing with somebody* for the best sales of the month. It takes skill to know when to use this, but when you do, it works extremely well.

## To Win a Competition

אכתריאל
אהיה
טככסירסיעה
דמב

AK-AT-REE-ELL
EH-YEAH
EH-YEAH
EH-YEAH
TEE-CHAK-ASS-AY
OR-OH-SAY-EE-HAY
DAM-EBB

# End Bad Luck

If you've experienced a long run of bad luck, this should be the first magick you use.

The powers will clear negative influences and help shift you out of your current situation.

It's possible you'll experience moments of intuition that give you clues about how to improve your luck.

# End Bad Luck

אהיה
צורטק
יאהבוגה
יפהזוקה

נגדיאל
זקפיאל
פקדיאל
גבריאל
סריגורא

EH-YEAH
TZ-UR-TAK
YEE-AH-HA-VEEV-GE-HAH
YEEF-HAZ-VUH-KAY-HAH
NAG-DEE-ELL
ZAG-FEE-ELL
PACK-DEE-ELL
GAV-REE-ELL
SAH-REE-GORE-AH

# Protection from Violence

If you suspect or fear violence, this magick can help protect you. It works whether you fear violence in general, violence from specific groups of people or even from individuals you know well.

You should always take real-world steps if you fear violence, of course. Get out of the way and call the police if you can. But for situations where you feel the need for supernatural protection, this magick is beautiful and calming.

# Protection from Violence

אדירירון
צורטק
ישהקווה
נפליאל לאו

ADD-EAR-EAR-ON
ADD-EAR-ON
TZ-UR-TAK
YEE-SHOO-HAK-OVAH-VAHA
NAFF-LEE-ELL
LAV

# Make Somebody Kinder

There are often people in your life that you can't get rid of, and don't want to get rid of, but you wish they would be kinder. This magick can soften a person's heart so that they are warmer to you.

This can be used to make a boss more lenient, a co-worker less negative or a partner more supportive. In any situation where you find yourself wishing somebody could be kinder to you, this will work.

# Make Somebody Kinder

אדני
ינהגודה
קפציאל
יחהקוכה אהוי

ADD-OH-NAY
YIN-AH-HA-GIVE-DAH-HAH
KAF-TZEE-ELL
YICH-EH-AK-EV-CAH-HA
EH-AV

# Make Your Money Go Further

Earning money is one thing, but holding onto it is even harder. In occult circles, it is regarded as wise to get out of debt, and then let money flow in and out of your life, but at all times it helps if you can make your money go further.

This magick will ensure that you get the best deal every time, that you always find bargains, and that 'mistakes' happen when people are selling things to you (to your advantage). It ensures that bills are smaller and that expenses are not as disruptive.

Many people perform magick to make money, but this magick can be just as effective for taking the stress out of your life.

# Make Your Money Go Further

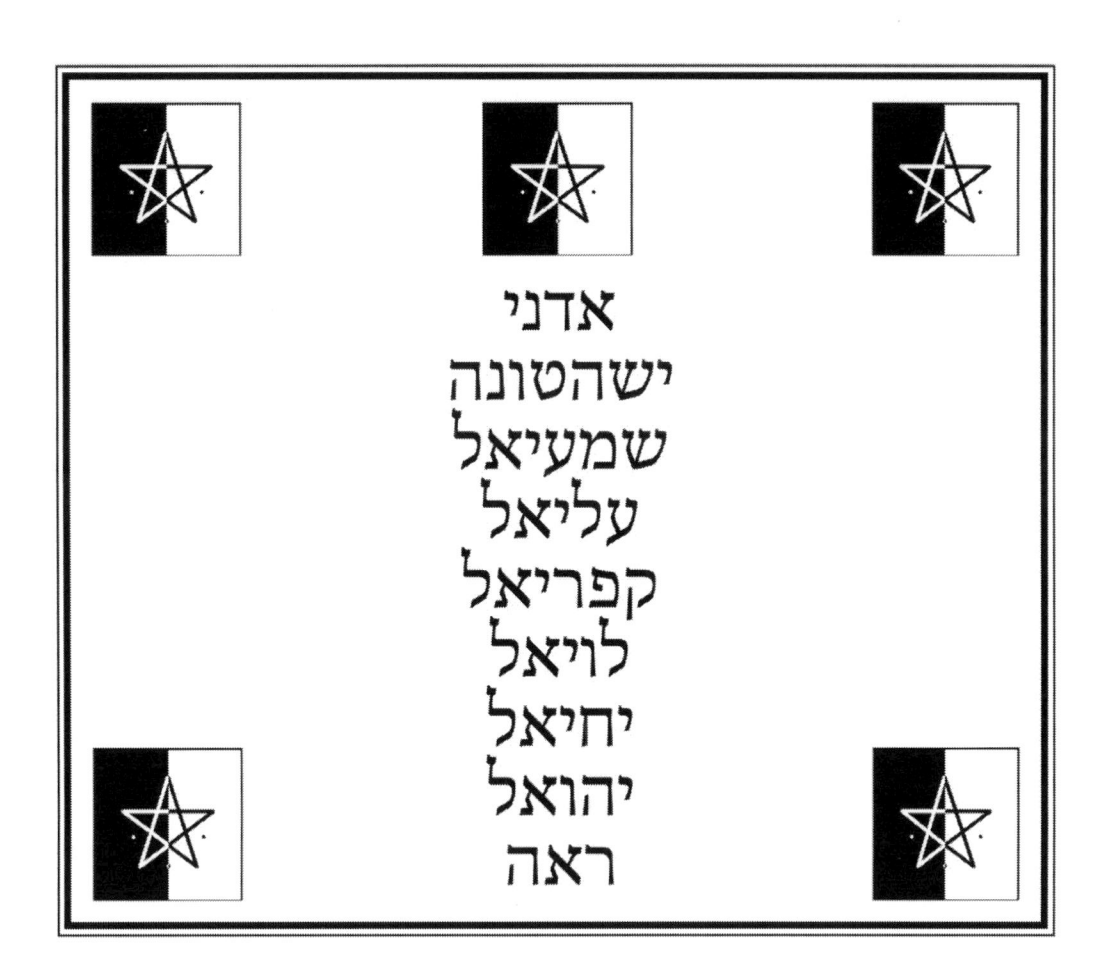

אדני
ישהטונה
שמעיאל
עליאל
קפריאל
לויאל
יחיאל
יהואל
ראה

ADD-OH-NAY
YEE-SAH-HAT-AV-UN-HA
SHEM-EE-ELL
AL-EE-ELL
KAFF-REE-ELL
LUH-VEE-ELL
YECH-EE-EL
YEAH-OH-EL
RAH-AH

# Attract Generosity from Others

There are two main ways to use this magick. You can perform a ritual to make people kinder in general. This means that friends, relatives, and strangers are more likely to be generous with their money. It can help when you feel that the people around you are mean.

The second way to use this is to encourage generosity from a specific person or group of people. This can be useful when negotiating divorce settlements, inheritance arrangements or any other kind of deal where somebody's generosity could help you out.

# Attract Generosity from Others

אדירירון
אדני
יאהבוגה
יחהקוכה
ריי נית

ADD-EAR-EAR-ON
ADD-OH-NAY
YEE-AH-HA-VEEV-GE-HAH
YICH-EH-AK-EV-CAH-HA
REE-YEE NEET

# Make a Project Go Viral

If you work in a business that relies on marketing, this magick can help your project to go viral. That is, news of your product, project, video, book or idea will spread wildly, increasing your online presence or sales.

When this magick was originally devised, it had nothing to do with the internet and was more to do with spreading messages that then began to spread by themselves, via word of mouth. We have refined and tested this for online marketing in particular. It helps if you apply this to something that has the potential to go viral – such as a specific image, video or product – rather than just to your website or business in general.

# Make A Project Go Viral

אדני
אכתריאל
יפהזוקה
נגדיאל
זקפיאל
פקדיאל
גבריאל
סריגורא
הקם

ADD-OH-NAY
AK-AT-REE-ELL
YEEF-HAZ-VUH-KAY-HAH
NAG-DEE-ELL
ZAG-FEE-ELL
PACK-DEE-ELL
GAV-REE-ELL
SAH-REE-GORE-AH
HAH-KEM

# Get Public Support for a Project

Sometimes, you want to get the public behind your project. You might be protesting against something, trying to raise funds for something else, or just want the local community behind your venture. If you ever want the public to support you, this is the magick to use, and it applies to global campaigns as well as local projects.

# Get Public Support for a Project

אהיה
יאהבוגה
עמם
הרח

EH-YEAH
YEE-AH-HA-VEEV-GE-HAH
OH-MEM
HAH-RACH

# Dedicate Yourself to a New Skill

In the modern world, you are often required to learn skills. The world has never been in greater flux, and your ability to learn skills quickly can make the difference between success and failure.

This magick can be used for work skills, or to improve hobbies, such as playing a musical instrument. It works by increasing your personal dedication, and ensuring that when you work on your skills, you do so with improved memory and better learning abilities.

# Dedicate Yourself to a New Skill

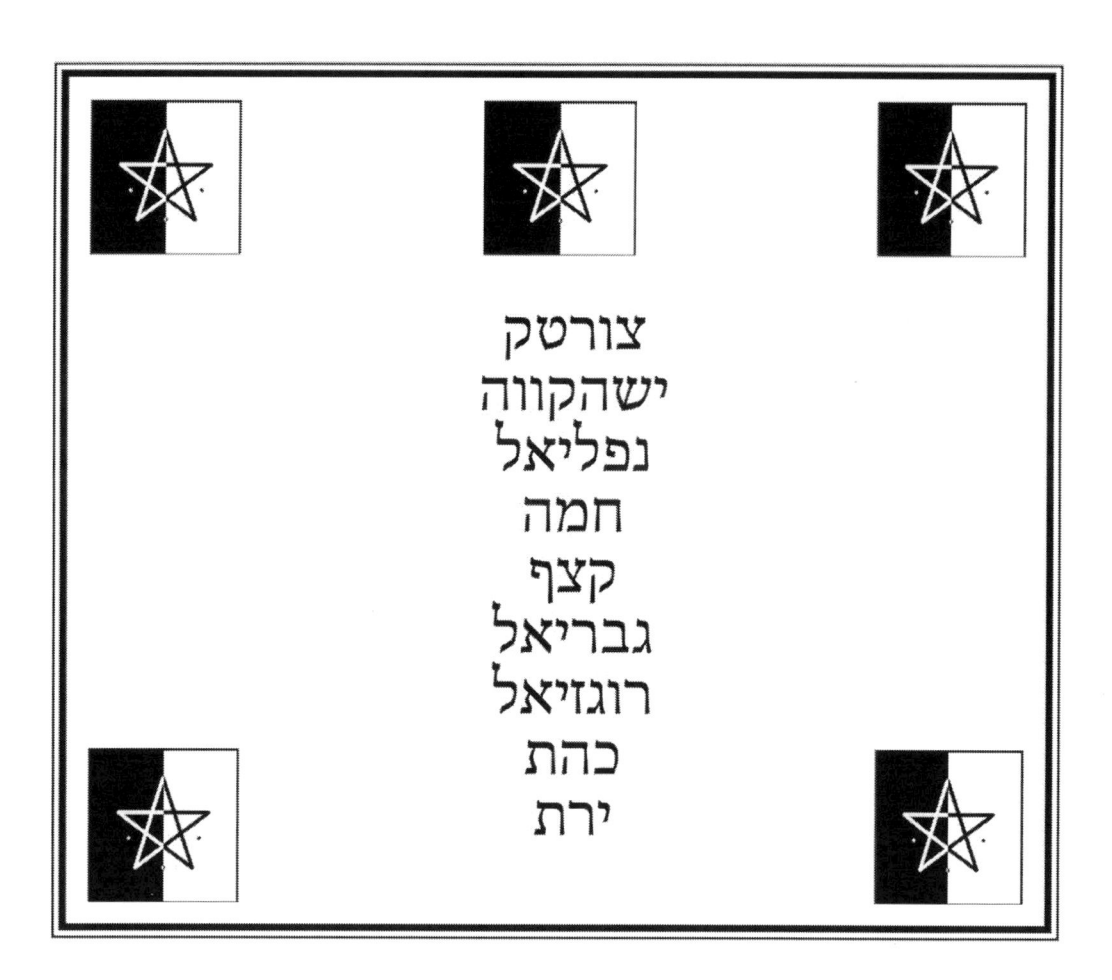

צורטק
ישהקווה
נפליאל
חמה
קצף
גבריאל
רוגזיאל
כהת
ירת

TZ-UR-TAK
YEE-SHOO-HAK-OVAH-VAHA
NAFF-LEE-ELL
CHEH-EE-MAH
KET-ZEF
GAV-REE-ELL
RAWG-ZEE-ELL
CAR-HET
YEAH-RET

# Obtain Wisdom

There are times when we don't know what to do, who to turn to or how to make a decision. If you are faced with a dilemma like that, use this magick to obtain wisdom.

The result may come in the form of intuition, a dream or just a gradual knowledge about the best course of action.

It works best when there is a particular decision to be made, rather than to make you wiser in general. So, if you are trying to choose between two jobs, two lovers or two completely different lives, this magick will help. A good decision can save you years of strain and effort, so this is one of the most powerful chapters of the book.

# Obtain Wisdom

אדני
יאהבוגה
אוהשירה
תזדיאל
נפסיאל
זכריאל
לויאל

ADD-OH-NAY
YEE-AH-HA-VEEV-GE-HAH
OH-ASH-EE-RAH
TAZ-DEE-ELL
NAF-SEE-ELL
ZACH-REE-ELL
LUH-VEE-ELL

# Know What Somebody is Thinking

If you want to know what somebody is thinking – whether they are a friend, co-worker or enemy – this magick will give you the revelation you need.

Sometimes you may be curious to know whether somebody likes you. You may want to know if an enemy has plans to harm you. You may suspect somebody of an ill deed, or you may suspect somebody of lying. This magick will not reveal the whole truth of any given situation, but it will let you know what a specific person is *thinking*.

This is magick that works well over time, when you want to gather intelligence about a person, but it can also be used in emergencies. I have often used this in business and personal meetings to discover what somebody is really thinking.

The results can come in several ways. Often you get a strong sense of intuition or hear the truth in a dream. Sometimes another person may reveal the truth to you, especially if your target has confessed the truth to that person at some point. At other times, the person may tell you what they're actually thinking, seemingly against their will. In 'emergency' situations, such as a business meeting, the result nearly always comes as a flash of insight.

# Know What Somebody is Thinking

צורטק
יחהקוכה
סודיאל
פתחיאל
עמם

TZ-UR-TAK
YICH-EH-AK-EV-CAH-HA
SWORD-EE-ELL
PAT-CHEE-ELL
OH-MEM

# Learn About the Near Future

Divination is a much sought-after skill, and many people consult tarot cards, runes, and even tea-leaves to get a glimpse of the future. If you want a more intuitive way to sense the future, use this magick.

It's best not to use it for reassurance. If you've applied for a job, don't use this magick to find out whether you'll get the job. Just wait and see. Instead, use this magick when you are trying to learn more about the future so you can prepare yourself and make better decisions when the future arrives.

The 'near future' refers to events that may occur during the next four weeks. If you want to know about events further in the future, use the next chapter.

Once the magick is done, forget about the magick, and before too long the result will manifest as a strong intuition, a dream, or a growing awareness of what is coming your way and how it will affect you. When you sense the answer coming through, try not to yearn for more detail, but observe passively, and more details will emerge.

# Learn About the Near Future

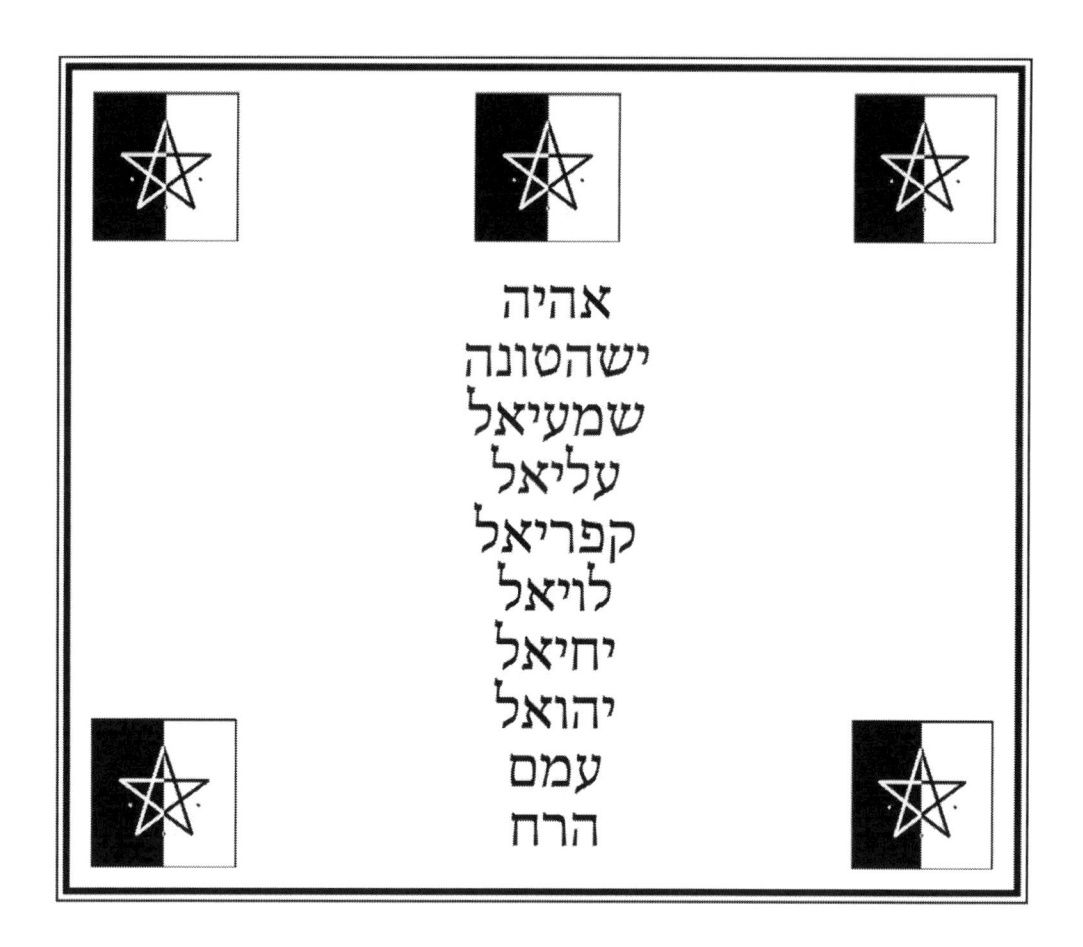

אהיה
ישהטונה
שמעיאל
עליאל
קפריאל
לויאל
יחיאל
יהואל
עמם
הרח

EH-YEAH
YEE-SAH-HAT-AV-UN-HA
SHEM-EE-ELL
AL-EE-ELL
KAFF-REE-ELL
LUH-VEE-ELL
YECH-EE-EL
YEAH-OH-EL
OH-MEM
HAH-RACH

# Learn About the Far Future

If you want to know about events that are some distance in the future, to help you make strategic decisions about your life, use this magick. It works particularly well when applied to relationships, but can be used to divine any aspect of your future.

Use this magick when you want to know about events that are more than four weeks away. You can look as far ahead as a few years, but be aware that due to the changes that occur as you progress through your life, answers are less reliable the farther forward you look.

As with the previous chapter, the result may manifest as a strong and instant intuition, a single word spoken by a spirit, a gradual awareness, dreams or visions. It can take several days for the results to come through, so forget about the magick and allow the result to arise when the spirits choose.

# Learn About the Far Future

אהיה
ישהטונה
שמעיאל
עליאל
קפריאל
לויאל
יחיאל
יהואל

אוהשירה
תזדיאל
נפסיאל
זכריאל
לויאל
איההיהה

EH-YEAH
YEE-SAH-HAT-AV-UN-HA
SHEM-EE-ELL
AL-EE-ELL
KAFF-REE-ELL
LUH-VEE-ELL
YECH-EE-EL
YEAH-OH-EL
OH-ASH-EE-RAH
TAZ-DEE-ELL
NAF-SEE-ELL
ZACH-REE-ELL
LUH-VEE-ELL
EE-YAH-HAY-EH-AH

# Become the Most Loveable Version of Yourself

Despite the description, this doesn't mean the magick will turn you into a cuddly and loveable teddy-bear of a person. This magick is aimed at making you seem supreme to others so that they are drawn to you.

The magick can be used in two ways. In the first, you focus on making the magick work to let your true beauty shine through. This allows people see your soul, and desire you for who you are, or desire to work with you because they sense your talents.

The second way to use this is to request changes in yourself. After reflection, you may decide that you are too lazy, grumpy and overweight, for example. Don't be too hard on yourself, but identify the things that make you less appealing to others and use this magick to encourage change. You must then follow through on the change with real-world effort, and the spirits will support your effort.

# Become the Most Lovable Version of Yourself

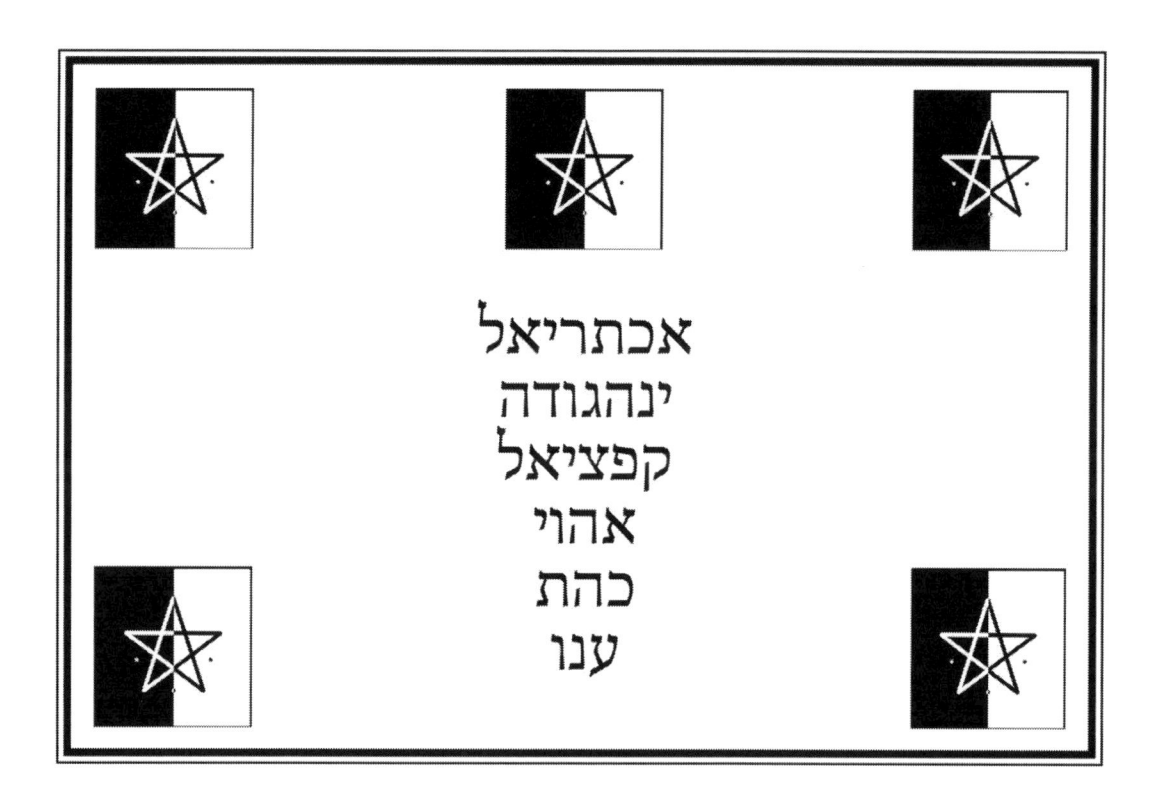

אכתריאל
ינהגודה
קפציאל
אהוי
כהת
ענו

AK-AT-REE-ELL
YIN-AH-HA-GIVE-DAH-HAH
KAF-TZEE-ELL
EH-AV-YEAH
EH-AV-YEAH
EH-AV-YEAH
CAR-HET
ANN-OO

# **Feel More Self-Respect**

When people have asked me for help with their magick, I often find that many people don't like themselves. They are trying to do magick to improve their lives, but have a low opinion of themselves. This means that even if the magick works they will remain unhappy.

Self-respect has many benefits. It makes you happier, more attractive, and more useful in group situations. It helps with confidence and makes your interactions with others easier.

This magick will not make you arrogant but will connect you to your true desires, your beauty and the light of your soul, enabling you to gain more self-respect. It can be used once, or whenever you feel bad about yourself, with results growing over the weeks and months that follow.

It can even be used in the middle of a situation where you feel your self-respect slipping – such as a date that's not going well - and the results can manifest instantly.

# Feel More Self-Respect

אדירירון
יאהבוגה
אהוי
ענו
ראה

ADD-EAR-EAR-ON
YEE-AH-HA-VEEV-GE-HAH
EH-AV-YEAH
EH-AV-YEAH
EH-AV-YEAH
ANN-OO
RA-AH

# Be the Center of Attention

This magick can be used for something as simple as a party or as important as a business conference. These days, networking is vital to success in most industries, and if you're meeting people in person (as opposed to online), this magick will ensure you're never left standing alone in a corner. People will introduce themselves to you and want to get to know you.

The only problem with this magick is that it can make you shine so brightly that some people will want to keep you to themselves. If you're networking, it's important to work the crowd and meet everybody of importance, so you will have to work to ensure that you are available to all the people who want to talk to you.

This magick has also been used by people who take part in talent competitions, or auditions, to ensure that they never get ignored.

The magick works best when there is a fairly large crowd and some competitive element to being seen.

# Be the Center of Attention

אכתריאל
ייהגולה
טוביאל
מיכאל
אוריאל
נוריאל
ידידיה
הקם
פוי
מחי

AK-AT-REE-ELL
YEE-YAH-HAH-GAV-LEE-HA
TWO-VEE-ELL
MICH-AH-ELL
OR-EE-ELL
NOO-REE-ELL
YUH-DID-YAH
HAH-KEM
POH-EE
MAH-CHEE

# Have Your Talent Recognized

When you've spent thousands of hours developing your skills to uncover your talent, it can be frustrating to remain unknown or unrecognized. I have heard from so many authors struggling to find an agent, actors trying to get a role, and job seekers trying to find work. This magick will ensure that your talent is recognized.

Remember that magick is only one part of a situation. If you are an actor, this will ensure the director sees your talent, but if you are unprofessional, late for your audition or otherwise rude, you won't get the role. The magick works extremely well to ensure that your talent is seen, but you must ensure that you work on all other aspects of the situation to get what you want.

The magick works well in all areas but is particularly effective for actors, writers, musicians and other creative people who want to have their talent recognized.

# Have Your Talent Recognized

אדני
אכתריאל
יפהזוקה
נגדיאל
זקפיאל
פקדיאל
גבריאל
סריגורא

לאו
אהרייה
הקם
מבה
חכמיאל

ADD-OH-NAY
AK-AT-REE-ELL
YEEF-HAZ-VUH-KAY-HAH
NAG-DEE-ELL
ZAG-FEE-ELL
PACK-DEE-ELL
GAV-REE-ELL
SAH-REE-GORE-AH
LAV
EH-HAH-REE-YEAH
HAH-KEM
MEB-AH
CHOCH-ME-ELL

# Appear Valuable to Somebody of Importance

This magick should be aimed at an individual in your life who has some sort of power to help or hinder you. You can compel this individual to see you as valuable.

Whether you are trying to get a deal, get a job, keep a job, or impress somebody with your work, this magick will ensure that the individual you target sees you as important to them. Sometimes this is more important than appearing pleasant, talented or a team player. Being seen as valuable is regarded by many people as the single most important factor for achieving success in the modern world.

The potential of this magick is not always immediately obvious when you first read about it, but you will come to certain points in your life where you need somebody to value you. When that time comes, this magick will make a difference to your life.

# Appear Valuable to Somebody of Importance

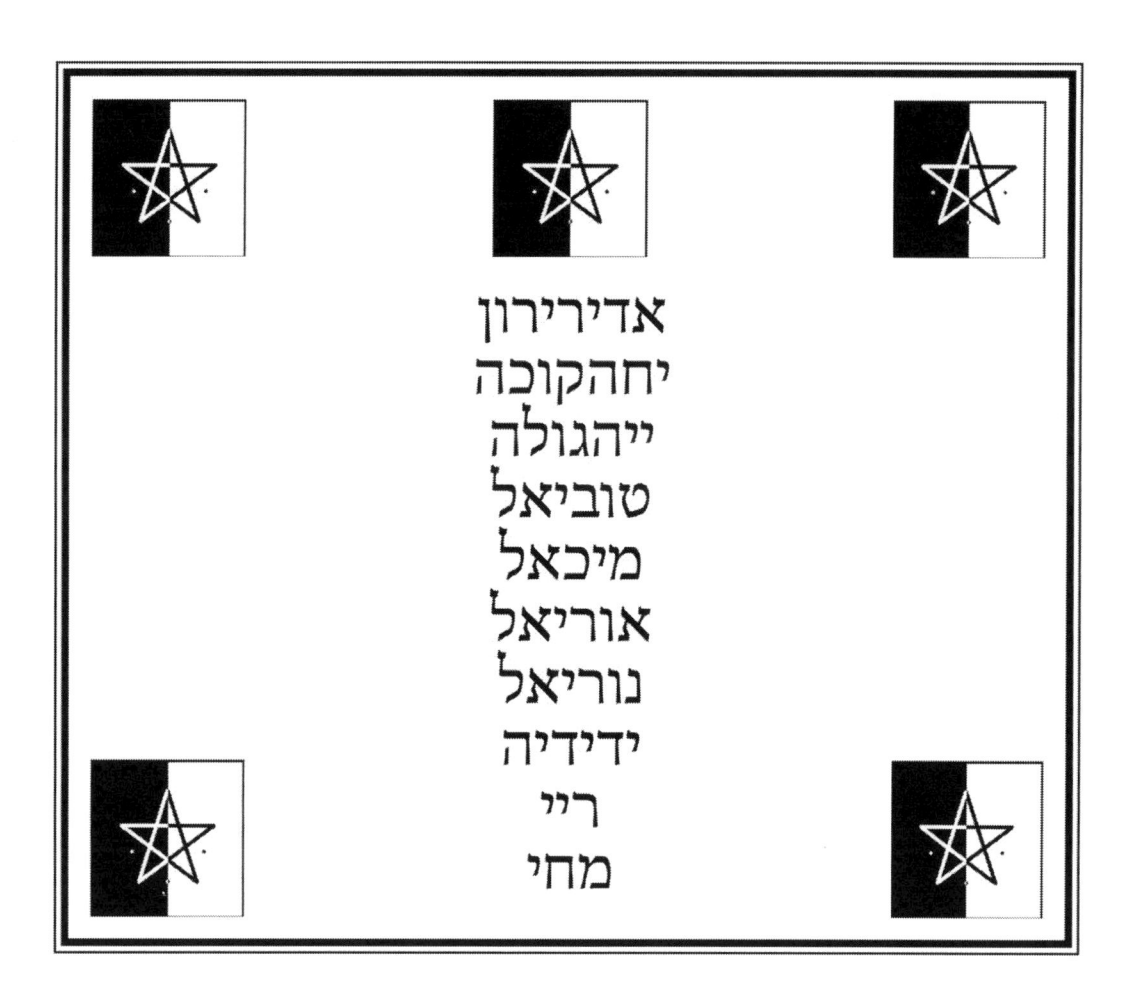

אדירירון
יחהקוכה
ייהגולה
טוביאל
מיכאל
אוריאל
נוריאל
ידידיה
ריי
מחי

ADD-EAR-EAR-ON
YICH-EH-AK-EV-CAH-HA
YEE-YAH-HAH-GAV-LEE-HA
TWO-VEE-ELL
MICH-AH-ELL
OR-EE-ELL
NOO-REE-ELL
YUH-DID-YAH
REE-YEE
MAH-CHEE

# Attract a Guide or Mentor

The most successful people in life always have guides and mentors. I have yet to meet somebody who was a complete loner and then made it to the top of their profession. I am not a hugely social person, but I still needed mentors in my various careers, and in magick.

When you know that you need a mentor of some kind, use this magick. You may simply want a better friend to guide you through your life, or you may want a professional mentor who can help shape and direct your career.

# Attract a Guide or Mentor

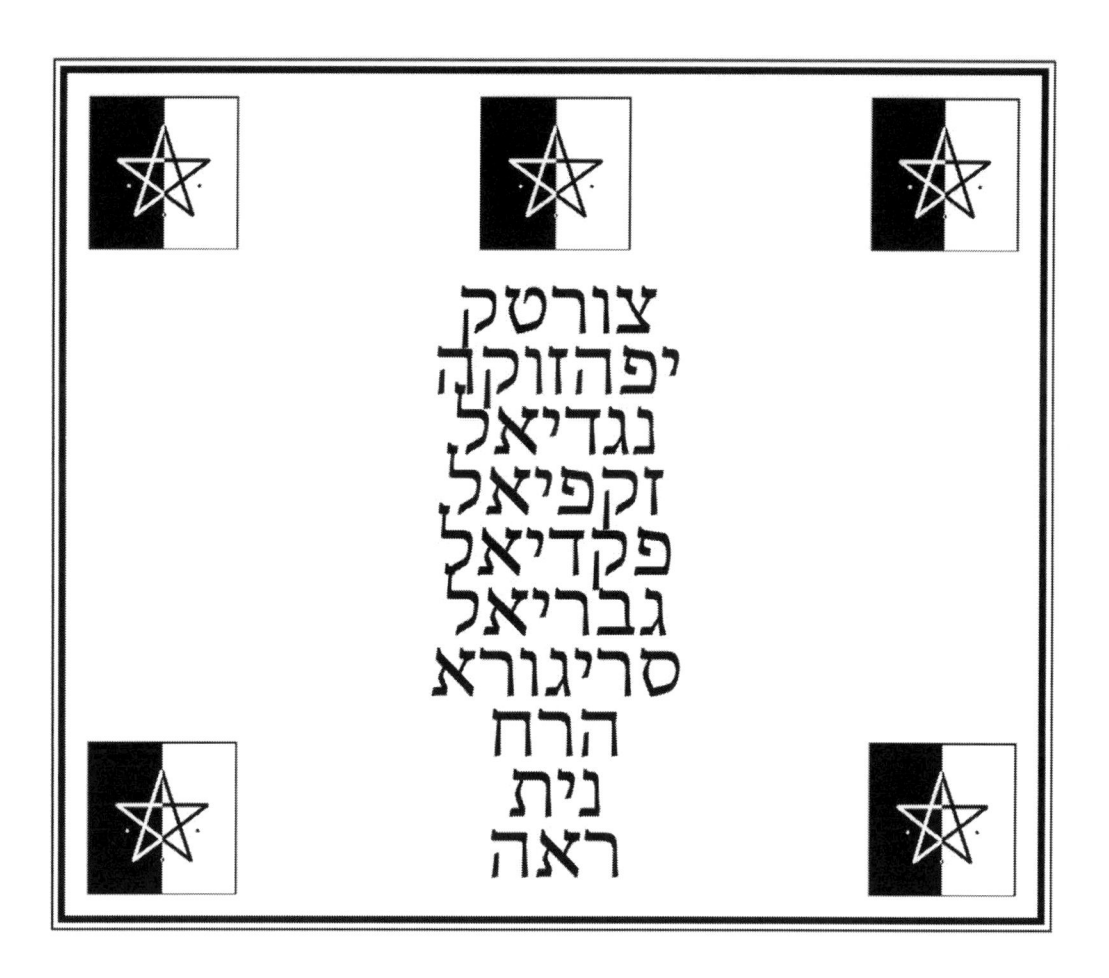

צורטק
יפהזוקה
נגדיאל
זקפיאל
פקדיאל
גבריאל
סריגורא
הרח
נית
ראה

TZ-UR-TAK
YEEF-HAZ-VUH-KAY-HAH
NAG-DEE-ELL
ZAG-FEE-ELL
PACK-DEE-ELL
GAV-REE-ELL
SAH-REE-GORE-AH
HAH-RACH
NEET
RAH-AH

# Be Given a Chance, Against the Odds

There are many times in your life when you are on the verge of success in a given venture, and you just need to be given a chance. This magick will ensure you get the chance to show what you can do.

I once saw this used by a man who wanted to date a woman who previously said she was not interested in a relationship. She gave him a chance, they went out, and things have worked out so far. I also saw a writer use this to get an agent to represent her, when the agent had, until then, said the writer's work was not commercial enough. And I know an actor who managed to get a director to let her audition for a TV role, even though she had minimal experience.

If you find yourself thinking that you need a break, and an opportunity to show what you can do, this is the magick you need. Be aware, though, that it only gets your foot in the door. The magick can give you access to somebody you normally wouldn't have access to, but it doesn't guarantee that they'll like you or your work, so prepare well and be willing to combine this with other Words of Power.

# Be Given a Chance, Against the Odds

אדירירון
אדני
ייהגולה
טוביאל
מיכאל
אוריאל
נוריאל

ידידיה
כהת
לאו
הקם
ערי

ADD-EAR-EAR-ON
ADD-OH-NAY
YEE-YAH-HAH-GAV-LEE-HA
TWO-VEE-ELL
MICH-AH-ELL
OR-EE-ELL
NOO-REE-ELL
YUH-DID-YAH
CAR-HET
LAV
HAH-KEM
ARE-EE

# Let Go of Guilt and Shame

In an earlier chapter I spoke of self-respect, and how many people are too harsh on themselves. In the same way, I find that many people are held back by shame and guilt. When you hold onto these feelings, they can prevent you from moving forward in your life, and they can even hijack your magickal efforts.

When you feel guilt or shame about a particular area of your life, use this magick. It may compel you to seek professional help, or it may just let the feelings clear away. Whatever happens, it will work to reduce or eliminate your shame and guilt. This makes you far more open to receiving magickal results and the life you desire.

# Let Go of Guilt and Shame

אהיה
יאהבוגה
פוי
ענו
מנק

EH-YEH
YEE-AH-HA-VEEV-GE-HAH
POH-EE
AH-NOO
MEN-AK

# Make an Enemy Terrified of You

Magickal attack is something that many people are uncomfortable with because they assume it will lead to magickal revenge or some kind of negative backlash. This magick can be used without risk, but only use it when you sincerely believe somebody is being unfair toward you. The angels employed in the working do not judge, and it is their duty to fill your enemy with fear if that is your choice.

This magick has many uses. If you feel that somebody is bullying you, insulting you or your work, harming your family or upsetting you in any other way, it is absolutely right to consider that person an enemy and make them fear you. When somebody is afraid of you, they will back away and be less likely to interfere with your life.

I have found this particularly useful for people going through difficult divorces. When one partner is bullying the other, this magick fills them with fear, and the bullying and threats come to an end.

It is best not to use this in some work situations, however, as a boss who fears you might sack you to get you out of the way. If it's a co-worker who's the problem, however, then this magick is ideal.

# Make an Enemy Terrified of You

אדירירון
צורטק
ישהקווה
נפליאל
חמה
קצף
גבריאל
רוגזיאל
לאו
ומב

ADD-EAR-EAR-ON
TZ-UR-TAK
YEE-SHOO-HAK-OVAH-VAHA
NAFF-LEE-ELL
CHE-EE-MAH
KET-ZEF
GAV-REE-ELL
ROG-ZEE-ELL
LAV
UM-ARB
MEN-AK

# Make More Time Become Available

Nobody seems to have enough time anymore. Most people I meet complain that they don't get enough sleep, work long hours and never get everything done that they want to get done. Despite their commitments, they can't find the time to exercise, see friends, travel or enjoy their hobbies.

In part, this is because of new social habits. There are some people who claim they have no free time but spend two hours a day on Facebook. In other cases, people may have overloaded themselves with commitments. For many, they are working every spare hour just to pay the bills. Whatever your situation, this magick works to extend the time available to you.

The magick works in many ways, and they are so varied that I can't list them all here. Sometimes, it may help you reduce a habit, such as the time you spend on Facebook. Other times it just makes sure you catch every green light. But the more impressive results are those that seem miraculous and time-bending.

When people use this magick, they often report that they seem to have more time, that things are achieved more efficiently, and that they have the energy to get everything done faster and without strain.

# Make More Time Become Available

אדני
ישהטונה
שמעיאל
עליאל
קפריאל
לויאל
יחיאל
יהואל

אוהשירה
תזדיאל
נפסיאל
זכריאל
לויאל
נית
ראה

ADD-OH-NAY
YEE-SAH-HAT-AV-UN-HA
SHEM-EE-ELL
AL-EE-ELL
KAFF-REE-ELL
LUH-VEE-ELL
YECH-EE-EL
YEAH-OH-EL
OH-ASH-EE-RAH
TAZ-DEE-ELL
NAF-SEE-ELL
ZACH-REE-ELL
LUH-VEE-ELL
NEET
RAH-AH

# Gain an Advantage, Obtain Any Desire or Find Favor

Magick that claims to give you 'any desire' sounds too good to be true, so this particular magick needs to be explained in detail.

There are three powers here. The first of these is to gain an advantage in any situation. If you are trying to outmaneuver somebody, be a better performer than somebody else, get more information than a competitor, this magick can give you the edge over your competition. It will not give you an overall competitive boost, but it will give you an advantage in one specific area. If, for example, you are a professional soccer player, competing against a team with great stamina, it might give you more stamina than usual, rather than the ability to score more goals. The important point is that you should not think about the result you want, only that you want an advantage in a particular situation.

The second power is used to obtain any desire. But the desire has to be sincere. You can't ask for something like a lottery win. This magick works best when you have a heartfelt and sincere desire that has been on your mind for some time, and when you are willing to let the results manifest slowly. I used this magick when I wanted to fly airplanes, as a hobby. It had been a dream of mine for years, but I never found myself with enough time or money to pursue that dream. This magick worked to provide me with everything I needed to make that dream come true. It can be used for obtaining a material object that you covet, for starting a relationship, for visiting a country, for getting a career you want or for becoming well known for your work. Use this magick on long-term desires that have been on your mind for years, and let the results manifest over the following months.

The third power is to find favor with another person. This should be used when somebody already likes you and appreciates your value, but you want to be the one they favor most of all. It works best in organizations and can be used to get a superior to favor you over others, or it can be used by a manager to get workers to admire you more than the other managers. In any place where you need to be favored over others, by one person who already likes you, this is the best magick to use.

# Get an Advantage, Obtain Any Desire or Find Favor

אדני
יחהקוכה
והו מיה אשל ערי סאל ילה וול

ADD-OH-NAY
YICH-EH-AK-EV-CAH-HA
VEH-VAL
YELL-AH
SHE-AL
ARE-EE
ESH-AL
ME-HUH
VEH-WHO

# When the Magick Works

The magick in this book works easily for most people, but if you find it difficult, The Gallery of Magick website and blog contains many FAQs, along with advice and practical information that is updated on a regular basis.

www.galleryofmagick.com

*The Gallery of Magick* Facebook page will also keep you up to date.

If you have an interest in developing your magick further, there are many texts that can assist you. *The Greater Words of Power* presents more sigils, using the same method as in this book.

*Magickal Protection* contains rituals that can be directed at specific problems, as well as a daily practice called *The Sword Banishing*, which is one of our most popular and effective rituals.

For those seeking more money, *Magickal Cashbook* uses a ritual to attract small bursts of money out of the blue, and works best when you are not desperate, but when you can approach the magick with a sense of enjoyment and pleasure. For those seeking more money, *Magickal Riches* is comprehensive, with rituals for everything from gambling to sales, with a master ritual to oversee magickal income. For the more ambitious, *Wealth Magick* contains a complex set of rituals for earning money by building a career. For those still trying to find their feet, there is *The Magickal Job Seeker*.

*The 72 Sigils of Power*, by Zanna Blaise, covers Contemplation Magic (for insight and wisdom) and Results Magic (for changing the world around you). Zanna is also the author of *The Angels of Love*, which uses a tasking method with six angels to heal relationships, or to attract a soulmate.

For those who cannot find peace through protection, there is *Magickal Attack*, by Gordon Winterfield. Gordon has also written *Demons of Magick*, a comprehensive guide to working safely with demonic power. Dark magick is not to everybody's taste, but this is a highly moral approach that puts the emphasis on using personal sincerity.

*Magickal Seduction* is a text that looks at attracting others by using magick to amplify your attractive qualities, rather than through deception. *Adventures in Sex Magick* is a more specialized text, for those open-minded enough to explore this somewhat extreme form of magick.

*The Master Works of Chaos Magick* by Adam Blackthorne is an overview of self-directed and creative magick, which also includes a section covering the Olympic Spirits. *Magickal Servitors* takes another aspect of Chaos Magick and updates it into a modern, workable method.

*The 72 Angels of Magick* is our most comprehensive book of angel magick, and explores hundreds of powers that can be applied by working with these angels. *The Angels of Alchemy* works with 42 angels, to obtain personal transformation.

Our most successful book is *Sigils of Power and Transformation* by Adam Blackthorne, which has brought great results to many people. *Archangels of Magick* by Damon Brand is the most complete book of magick we have published, covering sigils, divination, invocation, and evocation.

**Damon Brand**

www.galleryofmagick.com

# Appendix A: What the Words Mean

You can work this magick effectively without ever knowing what the words mean, but I gather that this makes many people feel uncomfortable, so I will make some attempt to explain how this works.

The rituals work by using combinations of divine names and angelic names. These are primarily taken from texts such as *Shorshei ha-Shemot*. We have a vast library of ancient texts and have studied those that we don't own in the great libraries of the world, alongside our own privately inherited collection of materials. The interpretation of these texts revealed the essence of the technique.

Some people ask why Hebrew is used so extensively in magick, and some will answer that it's because Hebrew is an ancient language, others that the Hebrew letters themselves hold divine power, and it can also be said that many of these rituals were devised using Hebrew, so they work best when performed in Hebrew. Whatever the truth, you don't need to be able to read Hebrew, because you use the visual scan and the pronunciations I've provided. This makes it work.

The words of the activation ritual are formed by voicing The 42 Letter name of God, which is found in some of the documents mentioned above. There are many debates about the exact vocalization, and the one I've included is one that works, which is all that matters

You will notice that the letters in the activation ritual, at one point, are spoken as KUH-RAH-SUH-TAHN. Some people have read this as Kara Satan. When you know that the Hebrew word Kara is 'to bow down' then it looks like you are being told to bow down to Satan, which would be alarming. But this misreading of the words only happens if you work with English approximations. Remember that the sigil is actually written in Hebrew. When you look at the actual Hebrew letters in the sigil, everything becomes clear. I'll assume you can't read Hebrew, but suffice it to say that the letters of the Hebrew word Kara (to bow down) are Kaph, Resh, Ayin. Those are *not* the letters in the sigil. The sigil letters are Qoph, Resh, Ayin, and these make the word Qara, which means 'to tear.'

Even if you can't read any Hebrew, you can visit these links, and you will see the second line of our sigil most definitely contains the phrase 'to tear'.

Kara, 'to bow down':
biblehub.com/hebrew/3766.htm

Qara, as used in our sigil, is 'to tear':
biblehub.com/hebrew/7167.htm

It should now be clear that the sigil does not say that you bow down to Satan, but it says, 'To tear away Satan.' Kabbalists have long held that this part of The 42 Letter Name means that you reject, remove or tear Satan away. The phrase is considered so holy that it is included in many Jewish amulets and chants for healing and protection.

It's all too easy to do a quick search on the internet and rapidly frighten yourself, but with thorough research, you can see that the letters used in the activating ritual are derived from The 42 Letter Name of God, and an aspect of that name suggests that you will 'tear away Satan.' By speaking these words, you align yourself with your true will and overcome evil, within and without. This is a safeguard within the magick.

But what does the rest of the activation ritual mean? This is something that remains open to debate, and I can't give a definitive answer, because there isn't one. You could say that it is a vocalization of the Name of God. You may look for meaning in Kabbalistic texts, and find that other meanings are ascribed to sections of the Name. In *Shorshei ha-Shemot* you will find that the name is split into three-letter parts, with various interpretations. So UB-AH-GEE has no actual translation but is related to removing conflict. TAHTZ is related to healing, and so on. This is why you get no sense out of it if you type the letters into Google Translate. These are not words as such, but strings of letters that have deeper meaning within a magickal context. Here, they work to activate the ritual, by activating *your* connection to this style of sigil.

What of the other words? Some are easier to explain than others. The opening words are always divine names, such as Adiriron or Ehyeh. The final word in each sigil is a Name of God taken from The Seventy-Two Letter Name of God. In between, you will find various angelic names and some words that are made by combining angelic names with other divine names. There are so many sources; you can imagine that explaining every detail would take an entire book five times as long as this one. All you need to know is that the secret combinations of these holy names and angelic names give you access to the powers described if you are willing to put in the sincere emotional work required to get results.

Hopefully, I've given you enough information that you can see these are not random words, or inventions, just because they don't appear in the standard angel dictionaries. Those popular angel dictionaries often miss out the content of more hidden texts.

If you have an academic interest in this, you can buy a lot of expensive books, and it can be fascinating. But if you want to learn about magick, *do the magick*, make room for it in your life and see the power it can bring you. Through experience you discover truth.

**Damon Brand**

**www.galleryofmagick.com**

Printed in Great Britain
by Amazon